Clydesdale Horses

ABDO
Publishing Company
A Buddy Book
by
Julie Murray

VISIT US AT
www.abdopub.com

Published by Buddy Books, an imprint of ABDO Publishing Company, 4940 Viking Drive, Suite 622, Edina, Minnesota 55435. Copyright © 2005 by Abdo Consulting Group, Inc. International copyrights reserved in all countries. No part of this book may be reproduced in any form without written permission from the publisher.

Printed in the United States.

Edited by: Christy DeVillier
Contributing Editors: Matt Ray, Michael P. Goecke
Graphic Design: Maria Hosley
Image Research: Deborah Coldiron
Photographs: Corel, Getty Images, Photodisc

Library of Congress Cataloging-in-Publication Data

Murray, Julie, 1969-
   Clydesdale horses/Julie Murray.
        p. cm. — (Animal kingdom. Set II)
   Includes bibliographical references (p.).
   Contents: Horses — Clydesdale horses — Color and size — Their bodies — How horses move — Feeding — Care of horses — Babies.
   ISBN 1-59197-306-6
      1. Clydesdale horse—Juvenile literature. [1. Clydesdale horse. 2. Horses.] I. Title.

SF293.C65M87 2003
636.1'5—dc21

                                                                    2003044308

Contents

Horses

People tamed horses about 5,000 years ago. Today there are more than 150 breeds and types of horses. They belong to three main groups: ponies, light horses, and heavy horses.

Ponies are the smallest horses. Most adult ponies are less than 58 inches (147 cm) tall. Shetland ponies make good pets for children.

Some children have ponies as pets.

Light horses are bigger than ponies. But they are not the biggest horses. Thoroughbreds and American saddlebreds are two **breeds** of light horses.

The Thoroughbred is a light horse.

Heavy horses have large bones and thick legs. Some weigh more than 2,000 pounds (907 kg). Heavy horses are strong, too. They are good at pulling heavy loads. Clydesdales, shires, and Belgians are heavy horses.

The Belgian is a heavy horse.

Clydesdale Horses

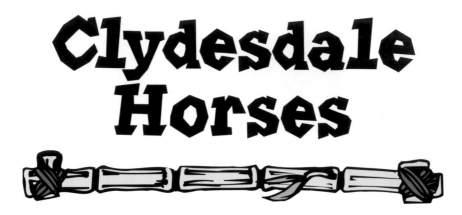

Clydesdale horses are gentle, friendly, and active. They have been around since the 1700s. Clydesdales are from southern Scotland. They came to the United States in the 1870s.

Clydesdales are draft horses. Draft horses are tall and heavy. They make good workhorses. Draft horses can pull heavy wagons and plows. Long ago, soldiers rode draft horses in battle. Today, draft horses often pull wagons in parades.

Clydesdale horses in a parade.

What They Look Like

Clydesdale horses may be brown, bay, black, gray, or chestnut. They have white hair on their legs and face. Some Clydesdales have a roan coat. A roan coat has white or gray hairs mixed with another color.

These horses have roan coats.

People measure horses in hands. One hand equals four inches (ten cm). Clydesdale stallions are commonly between 16 and 17 hands tall. That is more than five feet (two m) tall. They may weigh between 1,700 and 2,000 pounds (771 and 907 kg). Clydesdale mares are smaller.

Clydesdales move around on strong legs. On their feet are hard coverings called hooves. The long hair on a horse's neck and back is its mane. Clydesdales also have long hair on their legs.

Clydesdales have long hair on their legs.

How They Move

The way a horse moves is its gait. Horses have four gaits. They can walk, trot, canter, or gallop. Walking is the slowest gait. Galloping is the fastest gait.

A trotting gait is faster than a walking gait. A trotting horse goes about nine miles (14 km) per hour.

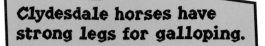

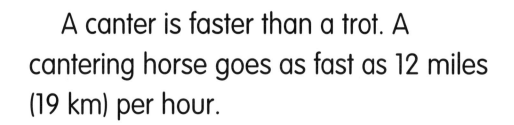

A canter is faster than a trot. A cantering horse goes as fast as 12 miles (19 km) per hour.

Eating

Horses eat grass, hay, oats, and bran. Adults need about 20 pounds (nine kg) of food every day. They also drink about 12 gallons (45 l) of water each day.

A horse's front teeth have sharp edges. They use their front teeth for biting. Horses use their back teeth for chewing.

This Clydesdale horse is eating grass.

Care

Horses have a lot of needs. They need fresh food and water every day. They need a large space for exercise. Horses also need a clean shelter called a stall.

Owners should brush and comb their horses. Brushing helps to keep them clean.

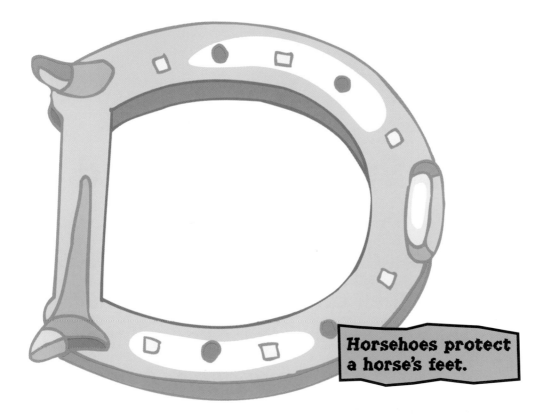

Horsehoes protect a horse's feet.

Taking care of a horse's **hooves** is very important. Owners should trim and clean their horse's hooves. Some owners put horseshoes on their horses. Horseshoes help to protect a horse's feet.

A Special Friend

Owners get to know their horses by spending time with them. Horses learn their owner's voice and smell. Through smell, horses know if their owner is nervous or afraid. A horse that trusts its owner can become a special friend.

Foals

Female horses, or mares, can have a baby once a year. A baby horse is called a foal. Wild mares mostly have their foals in the spring.

A mare and her foal.

Newborn **foals** can stand within minutes. They drink their mother's milk for about six months. Six-week-old foals will begin to eat other food, as well. Horses become adults after three or four years. Horses may live as long as 25 years.

Clydesdale foals grow to become strong adults.

Important Words

breed a special group of horses. Horses of the same breed look alike and share certain characteristics.

foal a young horse less than one year old.

gait the way a horse moves.

hand something used to measure horses. One hand equals four inches (ten cm).

hooves the special horn-covering on the feet of some animals.

mane the longer hair that grows on a horse's neck and back.

mare a female horse.

stallion a male horse.

Web Sites

To learn more about Clydesdale horses, visit ABDO Publishing Company on the World Wide Web. Web sites about Clydesdale horses are featured on our Book Links page. These links are routinely monitored and updated to provide the most current information available.

www.abdopub.com

Index